1

WARNING!
This book may cause you to have to change your underpants!

The **Dick and D[...]**

JOKE BOOK

This book belongs to:

....

....

So mitts off and go and buy
your own copy, cheapskate!

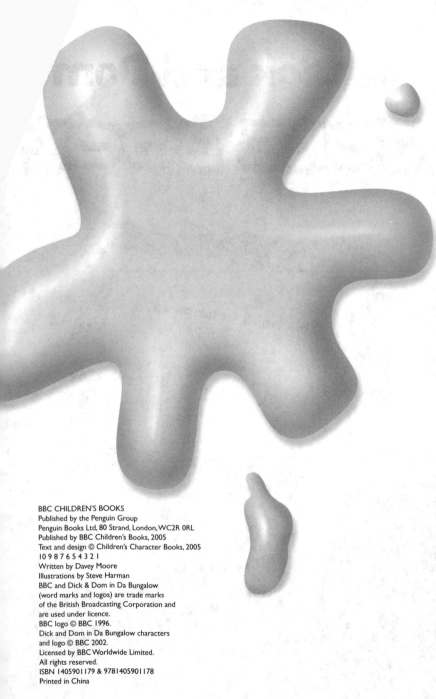

BBC CHILDREN'S BOOKS
Published by the Penguin Group
Penguin Books Ltd, 80 Strand, London, WC2R 0RL
Published by BBC Children's Books, 2005
Text and design © Children's Character Books, 2005
10 9 8 7 6 5 4 3 2 1
Written by Davey Moore
Illustrations by Steve Harman
BBC and Dick & Dom in Da Bungalow
(word marks and logos) are trade marks
of the British Broadcasting Corporation and
are used under licence.
BBC logo © BBC 1996.
Dick and Dom in Da Bungalow characters
and logo © BBC 2002.
Licensed by BBC Worldwide Limited.
All rights reserved.
ISBN 1405901179 & 9781405901178
Printed in China

Dear Sir / Madam / Idiot,*

Please buy this book for your brother / sister / son / daughter / grandson / granddaughter / niece / nephew / next door neighbour's pet labrador / yourself.*

Don't forget to pay for the book / have the book stamped / stamp your foot* before you leave the shop / library / your mate's bedroom.*

While reading this joke book, remember to make sure you have a hanky / box of tissues / bucket* ready in case you laugh / cry / throw up.*

We hope you enjoy this book as much as we enjoyed writing it, and that it makes you feel like laughing out loud / helping old ladies across the road / throwing things.*

Lots of love / hugs / buckets of slop,*

Dick / Dom.*

*Delete as applicable.

CALLING ALL BUNGALOWHEADS!

Dick

Welcome to our first joke book - the product of many, many hours of hard work.

YEAH, WE'VE SPENT AGES LAUGHING - SO YOU DON'T HAVE to.

In some ways, I feel this is something we've been working towards throughout our entire lives.

THAT'S RIGHT. THERE WAS NEVER A DULL MOMENT WHEN WE WERE AT SCHOOL. REMEMBER THE TIME YOU HADN'T DONE YOUR HOMEWORK, SO YOU TOLD YOUR TEACHER THAT YOU'D MADE A PAPER PLANE OUT OF IT?

And it got hijacked!

THEN THERE WAS THE TIME THAT OUR ENGLISH TEACHER ASKED YOU TO NAME YOUR FAVOURITE AUTHOR, AND YOU SAID, "DESPERATE DAN."

And she said, "But Desperate Dan hasn't written any books."

AND YOU SAID, "EXACTLY!" HA HA!

This joke book is my new favourite book.

THERE ARE lots of pictures in it. All
my favourite books have pictures in them
- even if I have to draw them myself.
Remember our school librarian? She was really strict.
SHE'D THROW YOU OUT OF THE LIBRARY FOR
THINKING TOO LOUDLY.
You were always late for school. Remember your
History teacher told you that you'd missed three tests
in one week?
YEAH, AND I SAID, "I MIGHT NOT HAVE TAKEN
THE TESTS, BUT I DIDN'T MISS THEM ONE BIT!"
Oh, yes, we did have a laugh didn't we? And all those
years you wet the bed, that's because you were
laughing so hard, wasn't it?
ER...YEAH. HEY, DICK, DO YOU THINK OUR JOKE
BOOK MIGHT MAKE IT ON TO THE BEST SMELLER
LIST?
Something in the air tells me it might, Dom!
Have you been at those sprout sandwiches again?
YES, AND THE PICKLED EGGS.
Eurgh. I think I'm going to be...

Dom

7

STICKY FINGERS

By now you will have noticed there's something funny about this book - no, not the jokes, the sticky hand on the cover.

WE WANTED TO GIVE AWAY A BUCKET OF CREAMY MUCK MUCK WITH EVERY COPY - THEN WE'D BE GUARANTEED TO SELL BUCKETLOADS.

Yeah, but buckets don't fit very well on bookshelves and we didn't think our book would go down very well in DIY shops.

No, it GOES DOWN A BIG HOLE IN THE GROUND MUCH BETTER.

So, then, Dom - have you got any suggestions of where I should put my sticky hand?

It just so HAPPENS I HAVE!

8

STICKY SURPRISE

Tape your sticky hand over the top of your bedroom door. When your Mum enters the room, she'll get a sticky hand in her hair!

Urgh!

CELEBRITY PICK UP

Cut out some celebrity faces from magazines and spread them out over a table. Stand a short distance from the table and flick your sticky hand at the pictures and see how many you can pick up.

That'll be a slap in the face for celebrities!

BOGIES!

SNOT FUNNY

Conceal your sticky hand inside your fist. Pretend to do a big sneeze and flick out your sticky hand like a big bogey.

Eurgh!

WaaaCHOOO!

Sticky Sauce

Next time you're eating out, stick your sticky hand to a sachet of sauce, salt or sugar. When someone reaches out for a condiment, snatch it out of the way!

Pass the condiments, luvvie!

what do you call a man who never uses a tissue? Greensleeves!

LEND A HAND

Sneak up on a pal when they're reading a book. Reach over their shoulder and see if you can use your sticky hand to flick over the pages of their book.

Handy Excuse

Next time your Mum asks you for a hand with the washing up - give her your sticky hand!

Talk to the hand!

How can you tell a snowman's been picking his nose? He's got stick-y fingers.

Sticky Forfeits

Write some forfeits on pieces of paper and turn them upside down. Mix them up and then take it in turns with your mates to use the sticky hand to pick up a forfeit.

I thought about having plastic surgery to look like a film star but I didn't want to pick someone else's nose.

What's the difference between sprouts and bogies? You can't get children to eat sprouts!

13

DICK'S TRICKS

School days are supposed to be the happiest days of your life. And if they're not, you might as well have a laugh about it! These tricks will keep you laughing all the way to detention.

Lumpy Jumper

Pull one of your arms out of the sleeve of your school jumper. With your exposed hand hold the cuff of the empty sweater arm. Hold both sleeves straight down with this one hand. Now the fun begins! Walk into class (or, better still, assembly) and alternately raise and lower your 'arms' and your hidden arm. It appears as if you are holding your hands, swinging your arms up and down while something mysterious is popping in and out of your stomach.

Sucker!

If your school serves milk with a lid and a straw, then ask your mate to go and get you a napkin. While she's away, take the lid off her drink and tie a knot in the straw. Replace the lid and act innocent when she tries to slurp her milk!

Cheeky!

When having a chat with a mate keep looking at a certain spot on her cheek. Look away and then look at the same spot again. Touch your own cheek in the same place while you keep looking. She'll probably ask you what you're looking at. Just say nothing and shrug. She'll probably be paranoid all day!

Sniff Out The Answer

Ask a friend, "What's green and goes backwards at fifty miles an hour?" When they say they don't know, do a big, snotty sniff.

BLEE!

with Next Door's Cat

Phew! I'm right tired, me! I've just walked all the way around the block. It wasn't very far though; it was only a baby's building block. Any road up, being as how I'm a cat, I've got a tale for you.

A weary traveller came across a monastery. The monks in the monastery saw that the traveller was tired and offered him some food and shelter for the night. The traveller had a good dinner of fish and chips. The traveller licked his lips and patted his full stomach. "Those were the best fish and chips I've ever tasted!" he said. "I must pass on my gratitude to the cook."

So the traveller walked around the monastery, following his nose all the way to the kitchen. (A good job he was following his nose, if he'd followed his bum he would've fallen backwards down the stairs. Or something.)

Anyway, when the traveller arrived in the kitchen he saw a solitary monk peeling a big pile o' spuds. "Greetings!" said the traveller. "I have just eaten the best meal of my life and I wish to congratulate the cook!" The monk looked up and the traveller said, "Are you the fish friar?"
And the monk said, "No, I'm the chip monk."

S'funny that, innit? I love chips, me. Eh, did you hear about the fight outside the chippy?
Three cod got battered...

DOM'S POETRY CORNER

Mother Nature is a wonderful thing. She has bestowed all kinds of gifts upon the earth for us to marvel at. Things like daffodils, waterlillies and industrial waste processing plants. Well, maybe not the last one, but they all move me to write poetry. It's safe to say though, over the years, one thing has stirred my senses, spurred me on towards great thoughts and inspired me more than anything else. That thing is...

Bogies

Some people think bogies are harmful,
But really, they are not,
When you think about it,
They're just dust - and a little snot.

My Mum gets really cranky
When I pick my nose,
She says, "Use a hanky!"
But I just use my clothes.

Sleeves are really useful,
If you want a sneaky wipe,
But you can't keep snot a secret,
As it leaves a silver stripe.

If you are close to someone
And you're feeling very cunning,
Rest your head upon their shoulder
And let your nose start running.

When my nostrils are a-tickling,
And I think I'm going to sneeze,
If I don't have a tissue,
I just "Ah-tishoo!" into the breeze!

I say "Yay, for sneezing!"
And "Hurrah, for snot!"
'Cause everyone who's got a nose,
Gets bogies - no matter what!

KNOCK, KNOCK!

WITH NEXT DOOR'S CAT!

Knock, knock.
Who's there?
It's me! Dick! Your comedy partner.

Knock, knock!
Who's there?
Cash!
Cash who?
What are you, some kinda nut?

Knock, knock!
Who's there?
Dismay!
Dismay who?
Dismay be your idea of a joke but I ain't laughing!

Knock, Knock!
Who's there?
Hawaii.
Hawaii who?
I'm fine, how are you? Now are you going to let me in or what...?

Knock, knock!
Who's there?
Ammonia!
Ammonia who?
Ammonia lil' kid and I can't reach the doorbell!

Knock, knock.
Who's there?
Ida!
Ida who?
Ida rung the bell if you'da had one!

Knock, knock!
Who's there?
Anita.
Anita who?
Anita stick so I can reach the doorbell!

Knock, knock!
Who's there?
Dozen!
Dozen who?
Dozen anyone ever just answer the door?

Knock, knock!
Who's there?
One stepfather!
One stepfather who?
One stepfather and I'll let you have it!

Knock, knock!
Who's there?
Apple!
Apple who?
Apple your hair if you don't let me in!

Dishes a great knock, knock joke!

Knock, knock!
Who's there?
Dishwasher.
Dishwasher who?
Dishwasher way I spoke before I had false teeth!

Knock, knock!
Who's there?
Spain!
Spain who?
Spain to have to keep knocking on this door!

Knock, knock!
Who's there?
Agatha!
Agatha who?
Agatha headache –
have you got any athprin?

I'M NOT SURPRISED SHE'S GOT A
HEADACHE WITH ALL THIS KNOCKING!

Knock, knock!
Who's there?
Alfred!
Alfred who?
Alfred the needle if you sew!

Ooh, it's that Mr Sew and sew again!

Knock, knock!
Who's there?
Iris.
Iris who?
Iris you'd come out
here and let me in!

KNOCK, KNOCK!
WHO'S THERE?
BEN!
BEN WHO?
BEN KNOCKING ON
THIS DOOR FOR ages.

Knock, knock!
Who's there?
Lisa!
Lisa who?
Lisa you can do is let me in -
I've been standing here forever!

KNOCK, KNOCK!
who's there?
Harry.
Harry who?
Harry up and answer this door!

25

Welcome to Pontypool!

DEAR Dick,

It's BEEN A LONG time NO SEA, BUT NOW I'm HAVING A lovely time iN Pontypool. I took A WALK ON tHE BEACH EARLIER AND SAW THREE ROCK pools. I tHOUGHt, "WELL, WELL, WELL." PoNypool HAS two piers. THERE WAS ONLY GoiNG to BE ONE BUt tHEY BUilt ANOTHER BECAUSE OF pIER PRESSURE. I BOUGHt SOME LOVELY SEASIDE tRiNKETS FOR DA BUNGALOW - I DiDN't HAVE to SHELL OUt VERY MUCH FOR tHEM. DoN't FORGEt to FEED NEXt DOOR's CAt!

Lots OF LOVE, YOUR pAL,

Dom ✗

(THAT's A MANLY KISS, NOt A GiRLY ONE, BY tHE WAY. MORE liKE A HUG, ActuALLY. OR, A HANDSHAKE.

Dick,
DA BUNGALOW,
NEXt DOOR
to NEXt
DOOR's CAt

No, A WAVE. OH, JUSt FORGET it.)

27

MUCKY BUCKET!

half-**BAKED BEANS** jokes!

BEANS ARE GOOD FOR YOU AND GREAT TO EAT - THEY'RE EVEN BETTER TIPPED OVER YOUR HEAD!

What kind of beans does a cannibal love? **Human beings!**

Hm, that sounds gore-juice!

What kind of beans are baked beans? **Runny beans!**

How can you stop Tuesday's school dinner from going off? **Eat it on Monday!**

WHERE DO BEANS GO TO THE TOILET? **IN THE CAN!**

These jokes are so old, they're all has-beans!

Baked beans, the musical fruit - the more you eat the more you toot!

Beans aren't fruit, fool! They're... er...like...beans!

28

Dom's No-brainers

Here's some really dumb fun to have with your mates!

Animal Antics

Write down the names of animals on some slips of paper and mix them up. Then make another pile of paper slips with some activities on. Try things like – baking a flan, riding a motorbike, leading an aerobics class, dancing at a party. Take it in turns to take two slips of paper and then act like a gorilla practising yoga, an ostrich going to the supermarket, a lion playing the recorder, or whatever. You can't speak, only make animal noises, while everyone tries to guess what you are and what you're doing.

Oooh! Oooh! Oooh!

IN THE DARK

Give everyone a piece of paper and a pencil and sit around a table – then switch off the lights! One person passes an object round the table and everyone has to write down what they think it is! Try a few unusually shaped objects such as a hairgrip, an action figure, or a piece of dried fruit. Keep going with quite a few objects before you turn the lights on. The person with the most legibly written and correctly named objects is the winner. Alternately, play the game for fun. Tell a spooky story with the lights off while everyone draws a picture to illustrate the story. See what crazy pictures you get when you switch the lights on!

Wooooh!

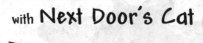

with Next Door's Cat

...I love fish, me. Make no bones about it. On a scale of one to ten I'd say I liked fish...oooh, loads!

Smell me breath, it stinks!

If I were a fish, I'd be a catfish. What kind of fish would join a monastery? A monkfish! Hey, listen, right – did you hear about the nun who got thrown out of the convent? Yeah, she had too many bad habits. Anyway, listen to this...

Sister Benedicta joined a convent with a silent order – that meant NO SPEAKING! The Mother Superior said to her, "You are most welcome here, but you may not speak until I direct you to do so."

So Sister Benedicta lived in the nunnery for five years before the Mother Superior said to her, "Sister, you have been here for five years now; you may speak three words."

So Sister Benedicta said, "Bed too hard."

"I'm sorry to hear that," said the Mother Superior, "We'll get you a more comfortable bed."

After a further five years, the Mother Superior called upon Sister Benedicta again. "You may say another three words, Sister Benedicta," she said.

So Sister Benedicta said, "Rough toilet paper."

And the Mother Superior assured Sister Benedicta that the toilet paper would be less harsh in the future.

On her fifteenth anniversary at the nunnery, the Mother Superior once again called Sister Benedicta into her office.

"Three words you may say today," said the Mother Superior.

"I'm outta here!" said Sister Benedicta.

"It is probably best," said the Mother Superior. "You've done nothing but moan, moan, moan since you got here!"

S'funny that. I got thrown out of a nunnery once, I did. Not because of anything I said though. Just because I wasn't a nun...

DICK'S TRICKS

in the cookhouse!

The kitchen — an area for preparing nourishing victuals while, perhaps, partaking of a pre-prandial libation. Also the perfect place to cook up a few larks! **Hurrooh!**

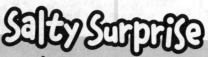

Salty Surprise

Cook up a batch of biscuits and replace the sugar in the recipe with salt. They'll look great but taste icky! Leave out your biscuits and wait for your victim.

Losing Streak

Wet the end of your middle finger and dip it into some cocoa powder or instant coffee. Tell your mate that he has something on his cheek. Point at his cheek with a clean finger while tucking your middle finger into your palm. After he wipes his face say, "No, you missed it! I'll wipe it off for you!" Reach up to their face and rub on the cocoa or coffee. This will leave a large smudge on their cheek. Your mate will walk around without knowing the smudge is there until he sees himself in the mirror — then you'd better make a run for it!

Water Mess

Fill a glass with water, all the way up to the brim. Hold a piece of stiff cardboard tightly over the glass and flip it upside down on kitchen counter. Carefully slide out the card. The glass should look like it's empty and has been left to dry. When someone picks up the glass to put it away, all the water will come splooshing out!

ACCUSING FINGER!

HE DID IT!

Someone launched an air buffet?

Use this handy hand to point out the culprit. Or you can always pass the blame if it was you, of course!

100% natural polystyrene!

Puddle monkeys!

Sprinkle these puddle monkey seeds into a puddle and prepare to be astonished! Even we're astonished, as we don't really know what they are.

Fake bottom!

Simply put this fake bottom in a bag or a drawer – hey presto! Empty bags instantly become full!

Cheeky!

FRESHLY BAKED BREAD SPRAY

Let this off around the house and stand back for hilarious results! One squirt of this and everyone will think you've been hard at work in the kitchen!

Amaze your friends and confound your enemies with these X-Ray pecs!
See bones through skin!
See marrow through bones!

Send off for a not free catalogue including all these tricks and many less! Just send one million pounds pocket money to: Dick c/o da Bungalow, Next door to Next Door's Cat.

Disappointment guaranteed every time!

MUCKY BUCKET!

MUSHY PEAS

Not suitable for grown-up consumption - kids only!

EVERY DINNER LADY LOVES MUSHY PEAS - THEY DON'T ROLL AWAY WHEN YOU DROP THEM SO THEY'RE EASY TO SERVE AGAIN!

Did you hear about the manky sausage that was made up of little bits of other leftover sausages?

It was called...Frankenfurter!

What's the difference between dog food and school dinners?

Dog food comes in dog bowls, school dinners come on plates!

Why was the cannibal sick after eating Dom?

Because you can't keep a good man down!

What's a mushroom?

Where you eat your dinner!

Mushy peas with poopy woo is a very popular dish...with flies!

Groo!

TOILET HUMOUR

with the Turtle's Head!

Ah, you've probably rushed straight to these pages. Well I can hardly blame you – they are the best! And by 'best' I mean stinkiest, so please make sure you wash your hands after reading. Oh, and if you get into trouble for saying any of these jokes out loud, just don't say where you read them, OK?

What happened to the thief who stole a lorry load of soggy sprouts?
He was on the run for weeks!

I bet he didn't make a clean getaway!

Did you hear the joke about the toilets at Glastonbury?
It takes a while to sink in.

34

When does
Q come before P?
During the interval
at the theatre.

What do you get if you
walk under a cow?
A pat on the head!

Remember!
A bird in the
hand... gives you a
mucky wrist!

Why was the stable hand unhappy?
His work kept piling up!

A dog saw a garden fence with a 'Wet Paint' sign on it - so he did!

Why did the tomato blush?
Because it saw the salad dressing!

WHICH FAMOUS ARTIST HAD BOTH AN INSIDE AND AN OUTSIDE TOILET?
TOULOUSE-LAUTREC.

Mum, can I lick the bowl?
No, you can flush it like everybody else!

what vegetable do you get in the toilet?
A leek.

36

37

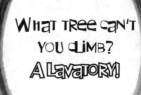

WHAT TREE CAN'T
YOU CLIMB?
A LAVATORY!

Why do you call your dog Carpenter?
Because he's always doing little jobs around the house!

Do you do the pools?
No it's Lady, our new dog, she isn't house trained yet!

Our parrot lays square eggs and it can talk. But it can only say one word..."Ouch!"

Why do stamps have the Queen's face on them? Because if they showed her bottom, no one would lick them.

WHY DID THE OCTOPUS BLUSH?
BECAUSE IT SAW
THE OCEAN'S BOTTOM!

why did the doll blush?
Because she saw the teddy bear!

Two pigeons were sitting on a park bench. The first one said, "What shall we do?"
And the second one said, "Lets go over to that car showroom and put a deposit on a new car!"

What do you get if you cross an elephant and a bottle of laxative?

Out of the way!

Use wind power – eat more beans!

DICK'S icky TRICKS

It's good to gross a few people out – just don't go putting anything in your mouth that doesn't belong there.

Funky Food

Liven things up at the dinner table, next time you have a mate round. Try adding a few drops of food colouring to some basic foods. How about orange mashed potato or blue pasta? They'll look weird but taste just the same! (Just make sure you're prepared to eat what you make, or you'll end up hungry!)

Sick Story

The imagination is a powerful thing! Remember this as you switch off the lights and tell your mates a disgusting story – and pass round the evidence!

Peel a grape and tell your mates it's an eyeball!

Pass round a knobbly bit of wood and pretend it's a bone.

A few breakfast flakes could be crunchy scabs.

Mash up a little cereal with some warm water and say it's something disgusting...! Even though your mates will know your story is completely ridiculous and made up, they still won't want to put their finger in a bowl of warm 'sick'!

Funny Bones

Put a piece of dried pasta in your mouth. Move your head from side to side as though you are stretching your neck. As you do so, crunch the pasta between your teeth for a gross bone crunching noise.

Potty Mouth

Shock your mates by pretending to eat something gross.

Chocolate raisins look a bit like rabbit or guinea pig poo.

Crushed up bourbon biscuits can look like soil.

Chocolate mousse, spread on the item of your choice, makes great poopy woo. All you have to do is set your fake dirt and then take a big mouthful when everyone's looking!

Don't put your finger where you shouldn't!

42

MUCKY BUCKET!

THERE'S NOTHING LIKE THE SMELL OF CREAMY MUCK MUCK IN THE MORNING!

CREAMY MUCK MUCK

Splash it all over!

How does an elephant hide in a bucket of Creamy Muck Muck? It paints the soles of its feet yellow and swims upside down!

What's yellow and dangerous?

Yeah, yeah, I know - a bucket of shark-infested Creamy Muck Muck.

No! Um...a machine gun painted yellow!

WHAT'S DOM'S FAVOURITE CARD GAME? TRUMPS!

Your mum smells a bit funny, today, luvvie.

WHAT'S YOUR FAVOURITE BISCUIT, LUVVIE?

It must have been that bottle of toilet water I gave her for christmas....

COCONUT MUCKAROONS!

SHAGGY DOG STORIES

with Next Door's Cat

...For a cat, I'm not much good at catching mice. I caught a cold once though. Terrible sniffles I had. I know how to catch a rabbit though, that's easy. You sit outside a rabbit hole and make a noise like a carrot.

I caught a fish once as well. Well, a can of fish. Dick threw a tin of tuna at me, see. And I caught it.

There's a couple down the road who are always throwing things – Mr and Mrs Spangle. They don't like the same TV programmes or the same food. He likes dogs and she likes cats – they just can't agree on anything. (Mr Spangle's not very nice. He spent a fortune on deodorant before he found out people just didn't like him.) Anyway, one day they had a row and Mr Spangle walked out and slammed the door so hard that a picture fell off the wall. He didn't come home that night. Or the next night. Not for ages. Twenty years later he came back and opened the door.
Mrs Spangle said, "Where have you been?"
Mr Spangle said, "None of your business!"
And she said, "Fine. Now hang that picture back on the wall in its rightful place!"

I had my picture painted once, by an artist. We had a game of football afterwards but it was very frustrating because we kept on drawing.

Which reminds me, what part of a football stadium is never the same?
The changing rooms! Ha ha ha...urgh...

44

DICK'S TRICKS Sleepover special!

Ah, a Bungalow-style sleepover – the perfect time to pull off some of your best pranks! Scarefully does it, now!

Eggy Moment

Next time you have a mate to sleep over, give them a 'boiled egg' with their toast in the morning. Just don't boil the egg! Sploot!

Don't Go There!

Make a big DO NOT ENTER sign for your bedroom and then see who dares to disobey your command! Open the door a little and balance a pillow on the top. Run pieces of sticky tape or a length of cling film across the doorway (if it's dark).

Alarming Trick

Pile empty drinks cans behind your bedroom door for a noisy alarm signal when someone enters your room.

Spider Scare

If you've got a mate who's afraid of spiders, tape a few lengths of black cotton from the top of your bedroom doorway. Tell her that you've found a whole bunch of big, black spiders in your room lately, but you think you've got rid of them all. Then watch your mate shriek as she enters the room and the cotton brushes her face like spiders' webs!

Wet Look

Cover the end of the cold tap with a little clear tape. Leave a little gap at the front of the tap. The next person who turns on the tap will get an unexpected soaking!

Cold Feet

Put a washing up bowl of cold water by the side of a mate's bed. When he puts his feet on the floor in the morning, he'll get a nasty shock!

THE PANTS PAGES

we love pants! where would we be without them? Chilly in the wintertime and in the Summertime... well, let's just get on with it shall we?

SPROUTS, BAKED BEANS, RICE

Dom likes to write his shopping list on his pants as you can see. And there are other things you can do with your pants while you're still wearing them.

Write the answers to any difficult questions anyone might ask you on your pants. You could start with your name – sewn into the back is good.

WEAR YOUR PANTS BACK to FRONT AND EXPERIENCE THE WINDS OF CHANGE.

Put both legs down one leg hole and hop into the bus.

Richard McCourt

PUDDING, CUSTARD, COTTON WOOL BALLS

In summer, wear your pants on your head to keep off the sun.

Put a torch down your pants and – hey presto! – your pants have become a talking point lampshade.

WEAR YOUR PANTS OUTSIDE YOUR TROUSERS FOR INSTANT SUPERHERO CRED – OR INSTANT DETENTION IF YOU'RE STILL IN CLASS.

what kind of pants does an artist wear?
Drawers!

WHAT DO YOU DO IF YOU
FIND AN ELEPHANT IN
YOUR UNDERPANTS?
WEAR ANOTHER PAIR!

WHY DID THE GOLFER CARRY A
SPARE PAIR OF UNDERCRACKERS?
IN CASE HE GOT A HOLE
IN ONE!

What did the twin dogs get
for their birthday?
A pair of pants!

What kind of pants does a lawyer wear?
Legal briefs.

Did you hear about the two fat men
who ran in a race?
One ran in short bursts; the other
ran in burst shorts.

49

What do you call a woman with baggy underpants?
Lucy Lastic!

What's the favourite game of a man with holes in his undies?
Draughts.

What wears a coat all winter and pants all summer?
A dog!

What kind of pants does a robber wear?
Knickers!

Cold weather is here, Dick.

Winter drawers on, Dom!

What kind of pants does
a big dog wear?
Boxers!

Don't throw your old pants away! Here are our top ten uses for old pants!

Use them to strain tea – or pea soup.

Cut them up to make handy-sized notelets for taking phone messages.

An old pair of pants makes a great windsock for a home science experiment – you could even call them 'windpants'.

use them as a duster

use them as a tea cosy.

use them to make a winter coat for your dog.

use them to make a balaclava for your Gran.

use them to make a hanging basket for plants.

use them to make a handy oven glove.

Boil them up to make stock for soup.

MUCKY BUCKET!

DIRTY NORRIS

extra mucky!

YET MORE FILTH BEING FLUNG IN YOUR DIRECTION!

What's brown and sounds like a bell? **Dung!**

Waiter, waiter! This coffee tastes like mud!
But it was only ground this morning!

How much do you think this bucket of Dirty Norris is worth?

What do you get if you pull your pants right up to your armpits?

I don't know, I got it dirt cheap!

umm...a wedgie?

No, luvvie, a chest of drawers!

Fast track your way to happiness with....

TURBOPANTS!

There's no need to second 'gusset' with these fly-fronted,
formula one-derpants! Their patented flame retardant lining
provides all the assurance you'll ever need.

TURBOPANTS – THE PANTS THAT ARE NOT PANTS!

Optional 'spoilers'!

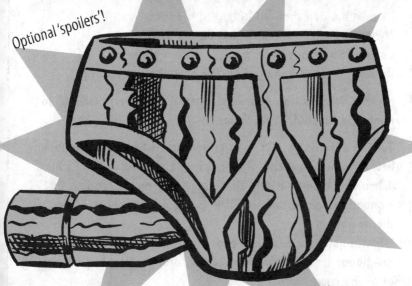

Go from a standing start to a flat
out run without leaving a trace!

Impress your friends, and be the
envy of nosy neighbours!

Your choice of design
includes - 'go faster' stripes,
'Number 1's,
or flame decal!

I never used to get
the girls, but now
I've got turbopants
I don't careanymore!

I've been wearing my
Turbopants for three
years - and now I'm
thinking of buying a
second pair!

NEW IMPROVED CHAFE-FREE FINISH!

SHAGGY DOG STORIES

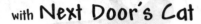

with Next Door's Cat

...I'm out of puff, me. I've just been chased by a dog. It was terrible, so it must have been a crossbreed – half terrier and half bulldog.

I know this dog that got bitten by a snake.
"Argh!" he said. "A snake just bit me leg!"
I said, "Which one?"
He said, "I don't know, all snakes look the same to me!"

He had fleas as well, that dog. I asked him where fleas go in winter and he said, "Search me."

Talking of dogs though...a man went to visit his new neighbour. They were having a cup of tea and nice custard cream in the kitchen and having a little chat about this and that when the neighbour's dog trotted in. "This is my dog, Duchess," said the neighbour.
"Has anyone seen today's paper?" said the dog. So the neighbour handed the paper to her, and the dog trotted happily out of the room.
"Woah!" said the man, "Your dog can read?"
"It's not that impressive," said the neighbour. "She only reads the comics."

Ah, that made me laugh that did! Listen, I just saw this old sea dog earlier on. I said, "How's the sea, pal?"
He said, "Rough!"

OK, so dogs go "ruff!" and cows go "moo!" – but what noise do giraffes make...? That's been troubling me since I was a kitten...

VERY SILLY JOKES

with the Prize Idiot

These are the prize idiot pages, so don't expect Shakespeare. In fact, don't even expect these jokes to make much sense. It's probably best you don't even them. Just skip this section. Or, if not, please don't laugh like an idiot.

What did one of the Prize Idiot's ears say to the other?
"Nothing can come between us."

Why was the Prize Idiot sacked from his job as a lift operator?
Because he couldn't remember the route!

I've got a giant pack of cards!
Big deal!

Why did the Prize Idiot eat a light bulb?
He fancied a light lunch.

Why did the Prize Idiot fill his piggy bank with currants?
In case there was a raisin interest rate.

The Prize Idiot went on holiday. I asked him if his tent leaked. He said, "Only when it rained."

Teacher: Simon, can you say your name backwards?
Simon: No, miss.

Did you hear about the karate expert who joined the army?
He saluted and knocked himself out!

What's yellow, brown and hairy?
A cheese sandwich dropped on the carpet.

What's the difference between poopy woo and a bar of chocolate?
I don't know.
In that case, I'm not sending you out to buy my chocolate!

Doctor, Doctor, I think I need glasses.
You certainly do, Sir, this is a pet shop!

Why shouldn't you try to swim on a full stomach? Because it's easier to swim in a full swimming pool!

How do you know if your mate is turning into a fridge? Open his mouth and see if a little light comes on!

The Prize Idiot had a job as a quality controller at a sweet factory. He threw out all the M&Ms with the letter 'W'.

Two snowmen are chatting. The first one says, "Can you smell carrots?"

The Prize Idiot hurt himself while he was raking up leaves - he fell out of the tree.

What happened when the prize Idiot tried tap dancing?
He fell into the sink!

Have you heard? The Prize Idiot has gone to medical school!
What's he studying?
Nothing, they're studying him!

Why did the prize Idiot drive his car off a cliff?
To check his air brakes.

What should you buy if your hair falls out?
A vacuum cleaner!

Two elephants fall off a cliff...
Boom boom!

A man walks into a bar...
Thunk!

Why do pens get sent to prison?
To do long sentences!

A cheese sandwich walked into a pub and said, "A pint of beer, please!" The woman behind the bar said, "Sorry, mate, we don't serve food!"

The Prize Idiot was going to go to night school, but he changed his mind because he couldn't read in the dark.

What gets smaller the more you put in it?
A hole in the ground!

I've got a pet amphibian. I call him Tiny - because he's my newt.

can you name a crustation?
Charing Cross Station!

What's white on the outside and green on the inside?
A frog sandwich!

Why was the prize idiot standing on his head?
He was turning things over in his mind.

The Prize Idiot put a lamp on his sundial – so he could tell the time at night!

Be alert! The world needs more lerts!

No, be aloof! There's enough lerts already!

Three old ladies went to the seaside.
"It's windy today, isn't it?"
"No, it's Thursday."
"Me too, let's go and get a drink."

The Prize Idiot's been happy
all his life - someone told him
a joke when he was a baby!

Did you hear about the stupid burglar
who saw a 'WANTED!' poster outside
the police station? He went in and
applied for the job!

Why do cows have horns?
Because they would look prize
idiots with bells on their heads!

The Prize Idiot sent his picture to a lonely
hearts club. They sent it back saying they
weren't THAT lonely!

Why was the archeologist upset?
His job was in ruins!

Have you heard about
the idiot who's going
round saying "no"?

No.

Ah-ha! So it's you!

Did you hear about the custard that
went to the disco with a bun?
There was custard in abundance!!

What do you get if you park your
frog on a double yellow line?
Toad away!

The Prize Idiot went to a fancy dress party
with a woman on his back. When asked
what he was supposed to be he said, "I'm
a snail." He pointed to the woman on his
back and said, "And this is Michelle."

DICK'S TRICKS

^ stinky

If you've got a messy prank to pull, and someone's going to make a stink about it, then where better to do it than the loo?

Toilet Terror

If you've got a nice and scary rubber creepy crawly then attach it to a length of cotton or fishing line. Tape the end of the thread to the underside of the toilet lid. When your mate lifts the lid, your creepy crawly will hop out!

> This works especially well if you build up to it with a spooky story about creepy crawlies!

Don't Loo-k Now

If you have a computer and digital camera then take a photograph of your toilet. Next time you have a gang of mates round, wait until one of them leaves to go to the loo. Then, gather everyone around your computer and open up the toilet picture. When your victim returns from the loo, he or she will think everyone has just been watching them on a hidden camera!

Toilet Accident

Tape a sachet of brown sauce to the underside of the toilet seat. Make a tiny hole in the sachet on the side of the bowl. Put the seat down carefully. When someone sits down on the loo, they'll unleash an unexpected squirt of brown sauce.

For a less messy trick, try the same thing but with a bit of bubble wrap. Gives a whole new meaning to 'just popping to the loo'!

What do you think of our joke book, Moose?

BURP!

Two piles of sick were walking down the street when one of them started to cry. "What's the matter?" said the first pile of sick. The second one said, "This is where I was brought up."

What's yellow and smells of bananas? Monkey sick!

What's the best way to talk to someone with bad breath? From very far away!

Nanny Nob Nob squeezed one out of me the other day – her hugs are too hard!

When you've got to burp, you've got to burp - and "better up than down," as Nanny Nob Nob always says. But it's not always appropriate. So here's our top ten list of the worst times to do a big, fat belch.

1. In your best mate's face - not that that's ever stopped Dom.

2. While having tea with Nanny Nob Nob - just not the done thing.

3. Right after eating fast food - it's like you're eating it all over again.

4. At the cinema, especially during a quiet bit - although it can be hard if you've had a jumbo-sized cola.

5. Just before you ask your parents for more pocket money - it's hardly going to charm them, is it? (Unless they're sneaky fans of Dick and Dom!)

6. During a prize-giving speech - unless you're the Prize Idiot, then a burp's probably the most sensible thing you can say.

7. During a chess tournament - you might accidentally rearrange the pieces.

8. During detention - if it's loud enough, you might get another detention.

9. During a live television broadcast - that'll be Dom again, drinking fizzy pop during the cartoons.

10. When you're just about to kiss someone.

ELBOW PILLOWS

Everyone knows where General Custer kept his armies – up his sleevies! But not many people know where he rested his elbows – on these hand-sewn elbow pillows! Custer didn't take his last stand lying down, he took it resting on his elbow pillows!

Buy one, get another absolutely free!

Available in three stylish colourways: camo, cheesecloth and denim-effect – all with contrasting piping.

ANT CROSSING

This handy rolled up crossing provides safe passage for your insect friends. Everyone will know when to stop while walking down the garden path – and because this ant crossing is portable, you can take it with you when travelling abroad!

It's a revolution in insect road safety!

TURN-UPS

Trousers the right length but otherwise lacking in savoir-faire? Then sashay out with these trouser-extending turn-ups! Turn-ups also act as a handy extra pocket for sand, biscuit crumbs and small pebbles.

NEW!

Literary turn-ups - printed with your choice of a Shakespearean sonnet or a saucy verse by Chaucer. Now there's a turn up for the books!

BIG POINTY FINGER

Do you sometimes feel shy when asked to give directions? Well, increase your sense of authority tenfold with this extending finger!

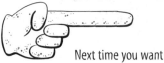

Next time you want to tell someone where to go, you'll really be able to show them the way!

OFF THE CUFF LINKS

Stuck for dinner party conversation? These novel cufflinks are a real conversation starter!

Also great for TV presenters stuck or making links between programmes.

Choose from the following designs:
My dog's got no nose...
Why did the chicken...?
Did you hear the one about the librarian with big hair...?

DICK'S TRICKS
dirty

Ah, practical joking doesn't have to be hours in the planning! Try these quick tricks and, if no one laughs or you get grounded at least you didn't waste much time!

Kickin'!

Liven up a long car journey. Put your arms down the legs of a pair of trousers and put trainers on your hands. Lean back in your seat and wave as you go by.

Fresh!

Put a couple of mints in your mouth and suck them until they've softened up a bit. Pretend to shuck yourself on the chin and crunch the mints as you do so. Then spit out your broken 'teeth'.

Ouch!

Walk quickly up to a door. Kick the bottom of the door with your foot but recoil backwards as though you just bumped your head, shouting, "yowch!" It works every time!

> That trick shounsh shimply shmashing!

Flushed!

Change a mate's answerphone message. Say, "Sorry, I can't come to the phone right now, I'm right in the middle of something." And then flush the toilet.

> I love a phony message gag!

Old!

Get up early and pick up the newspaper. Replace the middle of the paper with pages from the paper from the day before. Stick around to watch as Dad gets déjà vu!

MUCKY BUCKET!

SNOT

100% freshly squeezed!

IT'S S'NOT SNEEZY TO DUCK THIS BUCKET O' MUCK!

WACHOO!

What's a snot monsters favourite food? **A phlegm grilled bogie!**

Where do bogies go when they go on holiday? **Snotland!**

I wonder if they stay in slimeshare apartments?

What's green and smells? A FROG'S NOSE.

What's long and pink and comes out of DOM'S NOSE? **HIS finger!**

And a creamy muckshake to go!

Would you like flies with that?

My nose has gone on strike.

You'd better picket!

SHAGGY DOG STORIES

with Next Door's Cat

...I'm great at sports, though, me. Oh, yeah, I'll watch anything – bowls, darts, weight lifting, ice dancing. I never liked watching snooker much, though, until we got a colour TV.

There was kid once who was mad on snooker. He went to the doctor because he didn't feel well. The doctor asked the kid if he'd eaten anything unusual.

"For breakfast, yesterday, I had a couple of red snooker balls," said the kid. "I had the white one with a cup of tea for elevenses, and I had a black, a pink and a yellow for dinner. Last night I had a brown and a blue one for me tea with a couple more red ones for afters."

"No wonder you're not feeling well!" gasped the doctor. "You're not eating enough greens!"

I had a tummy ache once. I went to the doctor and I told him I'd swallowed a camera. He said, "Never mind. Just let it pass and we'll see what develops."

What's the difference between a camera and a sock? A sock takes five toes but a camera takes photos.

You can take my photo if you like. Would you like that? Shall I say cheese? Hey, what did the mouse say when it broke a tooth? "Hard cheese!"

That's hard to swallow, isn't it? Eh...?

71

DON'T DROP YOUR SAUSAGE!

Dick found this trunk of old jokes in the attic of da Bungalow and they're a scream! See if you can read them without dropping your sausage!

What do you call a person who rescues drowning spooks?
A ghost guard!

Why do demons and ghouls get on so well?
Demons are a ghoul's best friend.

Why is it hard to sleep in a graveyard?
Because of all the coffin!

Why are monsters' fingers never more than 11 inches long?
Because if they were 12 inches, they would be a foot.

Two big, ugly, hairy monsters were walking along the seafront and one said to the other, "Isn't it quiet for this time of year?"

What do you call a big, ugly, hairy monster with cotton wool in its ears?
Anything you like – it can't hear you!

What do you call a big, ugly, hairy monster with jelly and custard in its ears?
A trifle deaf!

What happens if a big, ugly, hairy monster sits in front of you at the cinema?
You miss most of the film.

What time is it when a big, ugly, hairy monster sits on your car?
Time to get a new car.

How do you know when there's a big, ugly, hairy monster in your bath?
You can't get the shower curtain closed.

How did the big, ugly, hairy monster cure its sore throat?
It spent all day gargoyling!

Why did the big, ugly, hairy monster have to buy two tickets for the zoo?
One to get in and one to get out!

Why are monsters big, as well as green and hairy? So you can tell them apart from gooseberries!

Why couldn't the ghost get to sleep? **Because he'd heard a person story!**

I didn't know you had a glass eye.

It just came out in conversation!

Did you hear about the mad scientist who invented an acid that could burn through anything? Now he's trying to invent something to hold it in!

Why don't cannibals eat clowns? Because they taste funny!

Why are monsters forgetful?
Because everything goes in one ear and
out all the others!

That's the 'eeriest'
joke I ever heard!

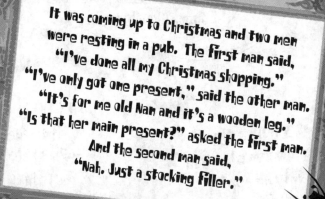

It was coming up to Christmas and two men
were resting in a pub. The first man said,
"I've done all my Christmas shopping."
"I've only got one present," said the other man.
"It's for me old Nan and it's a wooden leg."
"Is that her main present?" asked the first man.
And the second man said,
"Nah. Just a stocking filler."

Did you hear
about the cannibal who
went to a restaurant?
He ate the finger bowl.

What has 50 legs but can't walk?
Half a centipede.

Have you ever seen a man-eating shark?

No, but I once saw a man eating cod down the chippy!

What's worse than finding a worm when you bite into an apple?
Finding half a worm.

What's the last thing that goes through a bee's mind when it hits the windscreen of a car?
It's bee-hind.

I got into trouble for feeding the penguins at the zoo... because I fed them to the polar bears!

What's the difference between a butcher and a kid who's just seen a ghost? **One weighs a steak and the other stays awake!**

How do you know when a ghost is going to appear? **It's usually just before someone screams.**

Why did the ghost carry an axe? Because he wanted to get ahead!

That joke's so old it must have been made up by a crypt writer!

Why do ghosts make lousy liars? **Because you can see right through them.**

I'm looking for a monster with one eye.

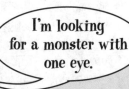

You're more likely to spot him if you use two.

This is my room, here.

Yo, Dom. Let me fill you in on all the latest goings on here in the bustling city...

Well, as you can see, it's been all go lately! Seriously, though, this city break is exactly the kind of holiday I wanted. Everywhere there are cars belching out smoke, and people - belching. I thought I'd have my face painted by a street artist yesterday - he drew two yellow lines across my fore-head. Still, at least no one's parked on my head today. I saw another artist who had a sign saying 'Heads neatly executed,' but I decided to give him a miss. Last night I went to the theatre. It was a terrible play - even the curtains were badly drawn. Later! Dick

Dom,
da Bungalow,
Muckington
- population: you!

DOM'S NO-BRAINERS

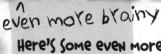

even more brainy

Here's some even more dumb fun to have with your mates!

STAMP IT OUT

Trust me – this game is a real laugh! Everyone has to tie a balloon to his or her ankle... Then try and pop everyone's balloons by stamping on them! When your balloon is burst you leave the game. The last one with a balloon is the winner.

Back a winner

Try running a back-to-back race. Everyone runs in pairs, with their arms linked at the elbows. Run to a marker – so one player runs forwards and the other backwards – and then back again. You will fall over, guaranteed!

I used to play this game with my old pop.

BRICKING IT

If you've got a bunch of bricks and a few willing mates, you can play this game. Everyone takes two bricks and lines up. They must race to the finish line without touching the ground - that is, standing on one brick while putting the other one in front of them, then moving onto the second brick and then picking up the first... And so on.

you will look like an idiot playing this game...brilliant!

FREESTYLE DISCO

Put on your favourite, liveliest music and dance around like a loon (putting your pants on your head is optional). Whenever anyone feels like it, he or she can shout "Disco!" and everyone has to try and copy what someone else is doing. It might take a while but eventually everyone should end up busting the same dance move. Then shout "Freestyle!" and go back to doing your own thing again. Keep going until you're all danced out!

SICK JOKES

What's the best thing to take when you feel run down? The number of the car!

When I was a kid, I swallowed a pen. My mum took me to the Doctor and he told me to sit down and write my name.

Doctor, Doctor, I think I'm invisible! Next!

Doctor, Doctor, I swallowed a whole cheese sandwich! **You must be choking!**

Doctor, Doctor, you must give me something for my head! How about this hat?

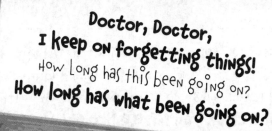

Doctor, Doctor,
I keep on forgetting things!
How long has this been going on?
How long has what been going on?

They say spinach puts colour in your cheeks, but who wants green cheeks?

Doctor, Doctor, I've got a split personality disorder! One patient at a time, please!

Doctor, Doctor, I think I'm a dog! Well, take a seat and we'll discuss it. I'm not allowed on the furniture.

The Prize Idiot had his head X-rayed – but it was ok, nothing showed up.

83

Doctor, Doctor, when I press with my finger here – it hurts! And it hurts here...! And here...! And here...! What do you think is wrong with me? **I think you have a broken finger!**

Did you hear about the thief who went to the surgery? The Doctor asked him to take a seat, so he did!

Doctor, Doctor, I have this irrepressible urge to cover myself in gold paint! Don't worry, it's just a gilt complex.

Did you hear about the bad tempered doctor with a short memory? He kept losing his patients!

Doctor, Doctor, I feel like a pair of curtains
Well, pull yourself together!

My Doctor took my pulse and told me I was regular as clockwork. I told him that was because he had his finger on my watch.

Doctor, Doctor, every time I drink a cup of tea, I get a stabbing pain in my eye.
Have you tried taking the spoon out of the cup first?

Doctor, Doctor
I feel like a needle
I see your point!

Doctor Doctor
I feel like a pack of cards.
I'll deal with you later!

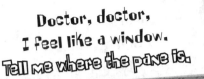
Doctor, doctor,
I feel like a window.
Tell me where the pane is.

I went to the doctor. I told him I'd broken my leg in two places. He told me not to go to those places anymore!

Doctor, Doctor, I keep thinking there's a fly buzzing round my head. Don't worry about that - it's just a bug that's going round.

Doctor, Doctor, I feel like a snooker ball. You'd better come to the front of the cue.

I was feeling weak so I got some strength pills from the Doctor. They didn't work, though. I couldn't get the lid off the bottle!

See! It bomb at the box office! Hear! The audience snore! Smell! The fear of the Studio Executives!

SEQUEL II

This time, they can see you coming!

"I laughed! I cried! For all the wrong reasons!" I.M.A. Critic, A Film Magazine

"Sequel II has all the action, all the spectacle, and all the romance, of the original Sequel! Except the original didn't have any action, spectacle or romance." I.P. Knightly, that free paper you get on the tube.

"I loved Sequel II! And so will you!" No-one at all, ever.

No animals were harmed in the filming of this dog – although a few hairs were singed on the Director's head at the wrap party.

Coming soon
– to a video remainder store near you!

BARGAIN BASEMENT

with Tom Dickunharry!

Awright me darlins! Tom Dickunharry here, with some top quality, honest guv'nor jokes that may or may not have fallen off the back of a Laurie. Yes, my friend Laurie, she always carries a rucksack full of jokes. Some people like to call these jokes 'old' but I prefer to call them 'classics'.

What do you get if you cross a footballer and a mythical creature?
A centaur forward!

Did you hear about the shy pebble?
He wished he was a little boulder.

What do you call a pile of wood?
A board meeting.

What position did the pile of wood play in the football team?
De fence!

Did you hear about the burglar who fell into a cement mixer?
He's now a hardened criminal!

What is never hungry at Christmas?
The turkey – it's always stuffed!

Parents are always telling you to act your age. And when you do – they tell you to grow up!

How can you tell if there's been an elephant in your fridge?
There are footprints in the butter.

Nothing makes me laugh like a good joke! And that was nothing like a good joke!

What starts with an e and ends with an e but only contains one letter?
An envelope!

Which two words in the English language have the most letters?
Post Office!

Did you hear about the overweight wizard?
He was known as the Lard of the Rings!

A piece of string walked into a pub and said, "A pint of beer, please!"
The man behind the bar said, "Are you a piece of string?"
And the piece of string replied, "Yes, I am."
And the barman said, "Then I'm sorry, mate, but I can't serve you."
So the string sat down, dejected.
A second piece of string walked into the pub. The other piece of string said, "There's no point coming in here, pal. They don't serve pieces of string."
So the second piece of string unravelled his ends a bit and tied himself into a knot and went up to the bar and said, "Two pints of beer, please!"
And the man behind the bar said, "Are you a piece of string?"
And the piece of string said, "No, I'm a frayed knot!"

You're having a laugh with these jokes, ain'tcha?

A dormouse walks into a pub and says, "Man, what a day I've had! I slept through my alarm clock this morning and my paper didn't turn up. Then I missed my train and I couldn't get a seat on the bus. And when I finally made it into the office. I realised it was Saturday and I was supposed to be playing golf with my old pal the field mouse. And then... Oh, a pint of beer, please." And the man behind the bar says, "Certainly, Sir – but why the long tail?"

Waiter, this soup tastes funny? Ah, yes, that'll be the laughing stock.

What did the tie say to the hat? You go on ahead and I'll hang around!

A bear walked into a pub and says, "A pint of...

...beer please, mate."
And the woman behind the bar said,
certainly, sir - but why the paws?"

WHAT CHEESE IS MADE BACKWARDS? EDAM!

Why did the man take a pencil to bed?
To draw the curtains!

I KNOW I really Shouldn't Speak with my mouth full but mmph umph ulumalammm.

Why did the orange stop rolling down the hill? It ran out of juice!

Why did the cowboy die with his boots on? Because he didn't want to stub his toe when he kicked the bucket!

How do you remove varnish? Take away the R!

What training do you need to be a rubbish collector? None, you just pick it up as you go along.

That joke was rubbish!

What's a hedgehog's favourite food? Prickled onions!

Did you hear about the cowboy who wore paper trousers? He was arrested for rustling!

Why didn't the banana snore? Because it didn't want to wake up the rest of the bunch!

I couldn't go to sleep so I went to the Doctor. He said, "Sit on the edge of the bed and you'll soon drop off."

Why did the baker get an electric shock?
Because he trod on a currant bun.

What might you win if you lose ten kilos?
The No Belly Prize.

Where do cows go on holiday?
Moo York!

What's yellow and dangerous?
Shark infested custard!

Two fleas were sitting on Robinson Crusoe's head. Just before one left it turned to the other and said, "See you on Friday!"

Ah, the old ones are the old ones...!

DICK'S TRICKS!!!
Dom's

Let's face it, most practical jokes are just plain mean. So perhaps you could tear this page right out of the book, give it to your best mate and say, "Go on, get your own back!" On the other hand, you could exercise a pre-emptive strike and get him with all these jokes first.

Ask for Dick

Phone a mate. When he answers, put on a voice and ask if you can speak to Dick. When he tells you that you've got the wrong number, apologise and hang up. Wait a while, then ring again. Put on another stupid voice and ask if Dick is at home. Repeat this as many times as you dare. Keep it up for as long as you can, maybe leaving a really long time between some of the calls. Then, when you think your mate is really going to blow, ring up one last time. When he picks up the phone, say, "Hi, this is Dick – have there been any calls for me?"

> Clearly this trick does not work if your friend is called Dick. Did I really need to say that?

Lighten up

Next time your parents buy something that comes in a great big box, seal the box up with tape and carry it round to a mate's house. When your mate comes to the door, make out that the box is really heavy. Do lots of grunting and straining as you lift it with great difficulty through the door. Tell your mate that the box contains a surprise for him and he'd better carry it upstairs. When he goes to pick up the 'heavy' box, he'll get a real surprise – and probably fall over!

> What dog is made of card? A Boxer Dog!

Snow in Summer

Use a hole punch to make hundreds of little circles of paper. Save 'em up and put them in a place where an unexpected 'snow' shower will cause a laugh. You could put them in a closed umbrella. Or in a mate's hoodie, but not if they can beat you in a fight.

BIG POINTLESS HEADLINE!

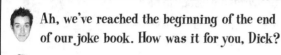

Ah, we've reached the beginning of the end of our joke book. How was it for you, Dick?

It was a laugh.

Only one thing is still troubling me, Dick. Do you like me?

Sometimes.

How do you mean?

The times when you're away.

Very funny, Dick.

Look, I like you enough to let you have the last word. What do you think it should be?

Oooh, I don't know. That's pretty hard, I'll have to think about it. This is quite important, isn't it? I mean, whatever the last work of the book is, that will be the thing that will really stay in peoples' minds as they put the book down and go off to do something else. So it should be something fundamental to us, something that really sums up our philosophy. Maybe something like, "And to all a goodnight," or "Where have all the flowers gone?" Or...

Bogies!!!